AFRICAN AMERICAN INVENTORS & SCIENTISTS

AFRICAN AMERICAN
INVENTORS &
SCIENTISTS

EDITED BY JOANNE RANDOLPH

Enslow Publishing
101 W. 23rd Street
Suite 240
New York, NY 10011
USA

enslow.com

PIONEERING
AFRICAN
AMERICANS

This edition published in 2018 by
Enslow Publishing, LLC.
101 W. 23rd Street, Suite 240
New York, NY 10011

Library of Congress Cataloging-in-Publication Data

Names: Randolph, Joanne, editor.
Title: African American inventors & scientists / edited by Joanne Randolph.
Description: New York, NY : Enslow Publishing, 2018. | Series: Pioneering African Americans | Includes bibliographical references and index. | Audience: Grades 5–8.
Identifiers: LCCN 2017018156| ISBN 9780766092488 (library bound) | ISBN 9780766093874 (pbk.) | ISBN 9780766093881 (6 pack)
Subjects: LCSH: African American inventors—Biography—Juvenile literature. | African American scientists—Biography—Juvenile literature.
Classification: LCC T39 .A394 2017 | DDC 509.2/396073—dc23
LC record available at https://lccn.loc.gov/2017018156

Printed in the United States of America

To Our Readers: We have done our best to make sure all website addresses in this book were active and appropriate when we went to press. However, the author and the publisher have no control over and assume no liability for the material available on those websites or on any websites they may link to. Any comments or suggestions can be sent by email to customerservice@enslow.com.

Photos Credits: Cover, p. 3 Nicholas Kamm/AFP/Getty Images; p. 7 Smith Collection/Gado/Archive Photos/Getty Images; p. 8 Art Collection 3/Alamy Stock Photo; pp. 11, 28, 29, 41, 44 Library of Congress Prints and Photographs Division; p. 12 AFP/Getty Images; p. 15 Michael Maslan/Corbis Historical/Getty Images; p. 16 BLM Collection/Alamy Stock Photo; p. 18 Science History Images/Alamy Stock Photo; p. 22 Everett Historical/Shutterstock.com; p. 23 Brian Stansberry/Wikimedia Commons/File:Knoxville-college-mckee-tn1.jpg/CC BY 3.0; p. 24 Michael Ochs Archives/Getty Images; p. 26 Library of Congress Newspaper and Periodicals Reading Room; p. 30 Bettmann/Getty Images; p. 32 MPI/Archive Photos/Getty Images; p. 33 Donaldson Collection/Michael Ochs Archives/Getty Images; p. 36 Robert Sullivan/AFP/Getty Images; p. 39 Fotosearch/Archive Photos/Getty Images; p. 43 Clevelander96/Wikipedia/File:Morgan signal.jpg; interior pages borders and corners fotohunter/shutterstock.com.

Article Credits: Richard L. Mattis, "The First 1,000 Inventions," *Cobblestone*; Heather M. Hopkins, "Seeking Equality in the Lab," *Footsteps*; Diana Childress, "One Invention at a Time," *Footsteps*; Diana Childress, "Lewis Temple," *Footsteps*; Robin Spevacek, "Madam C. J. Walker," *Cricket*; Karen E. Hong, "The Wizard of Tuskegee," *Footsteps*; Heather M. Hopkins, "The Sky's the Limit," *Footsteps*; Richard L. Mattis, "Big Chief Mason," *Cobblestone*.

CONTENTS

CHAPTER ONE

THE FIRST 1,000 INVENTIONS

I n 1903 a man running for Congress in Maryland made a speech. He told his audience that African Americans should not be permitted to vote because they were not smart enough. As proof, the man claimed that no African American had ever invented anything.

PATENTS AND PREJUDICE

Henry E. Baker knew better. He was an assistant patent examiner for the US Patent Office and was himself an African American. He had already published a list of three hundred seventy inventions by about two hundred African Americans through the year 1900. In that year, the Patent Office had conducted a survey to gather information about black inventors and their inventions. Commissioner of Patents Charles H. Duell had signed the survey letters, but Baker had done most of the work. He mailed the letters to patent attorneys, company presidents, newspaper editors, and prominent African Americans. He recorded the replies and followed up on leads. The black inventors were featured in a "Negro Exhibit" for the international Paris Exposition of 1900. The survey was necessary because nearly all the official Patent Office records said nothing about the race of the many inventors. Only Henry Blair was identified in the records as "a colored man." He patented a corn planter in 1834 and a cotton planter in 1836.

Blair must have been a "free person of color" rather than a slave because a slave could not obtain a patent. It is likely that slaves did invent things to make their daily work easier, but the records of these inventions are lost. Some masters may have taken their slaves' ideas and patented them themselves. The real inventor never got any credit. Some historians believe that Eli Whitney based his cotton gin on a slave's design.

Several other free African Americans obtained patents before the Civil War. Sometime before he died in 1842, James Forten patented a device for handling the sails of ships. In 1846 Norbert Rillieux (pronounced nor-BARE ree-YER) invented a vacuum evaporator for refining sugar. Sugar makers still use his process for removing the water from sugar cane juice.

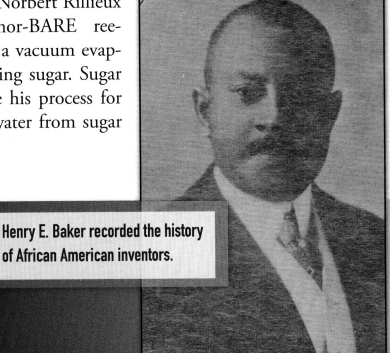

Henry E. Baker recorded the history of African American inventors.

James Forten (1766–1842) was a sailmaker, abolitionist, and wealthy businessman in Philadelphia.

The first African American who obtained a patent was Thomas L. Jennings, a tailor in New York City. In 1821 he developed a method for dry-cleaning clothing. John Quincy Adams signed Jennings's patent certificate, and Jennings proudly displayed the framed document in his home.

After the Civil War and the freeing of the slaves, the number of inventions by African Americans increased. Jan Matzeliger's lasting machine attached the upper portion of a shoe to its sole, a task that had always been done by hand. The savings in labor cut the cost of shoes in half. Granville Woods's many electrical creations led people to compare him to Thomas Edison. His inventions include a brake system for railroad trains, a telegraph between moving trains, and a train for an amusement park.

AFRICAN AMERICAN WOMEN INVENTORS

Henry Baker's survey also identified several black women inventors. Judy W. Reed probably could not write her name, but she patented a hand-operated machine for kneading and rolling dough in 1884. The following year, Sarah E. Goode patented a bed that folded into a cabinet that could serve as a desk.

In 1888 Miriam E. Benjamin patented a chair with a signaling device on it. When the person seated pressed a button, a bell sounded and a red signal appeared on the back of the chair. The House of Representatives adopted her invention. Congressmen could get the attention of their pages without calling to them or clapping their hands.

In 1892 Sarah Boone patented an ironing board that was especially suited to ironing women's clothes. In 1898 Lyda D. Newman patented a hairbrush that came apart for easy cleaning. Baker was pleased to discover so much talent. But he also realized that many black inventors would never be known. Some people who answered the survey had not kept accurate records. Some African Americans did not get patents because they could not afford an attorney. Some kept their race a secret, fearing that they would make less money if people knew that the idea had come from an African American.

The Patent Office conducted a second survey in 1913. The new information raised the number of known patents by African Americans to more than a thousand. Baker compiled a four-volume book on patents by black inventors.

SEEKING EQUALITY IN THE LAB

What makes these brilliant African American inventors even more extraordinary is the fact that they had to conduct their work without the advantages of state-of-art laboratories and equipment afforded to their white peers.

Even after Congress passed the Thirteenth and Fourteenth Amendments (abolishing slavery and granting all Americans equal protection under the law) in the 1860s, black scientists were held back by the misguided belief that blacks were not as intelligent as whites. Black scientists had challenged this idea for decades. In 1791 mathematician and astronomer Benjamin Banneker wrote a letter to Thomas Jefferson declaring the myth of black inferiority "absurd and false." To prove his competence, Banneker enclosed a copy of his widely used almanac. Impressed, Jefferson sent the almanac to the Academy of Sciences in Paris to show that African Americans were capable of science. Yet, many Americans continued to believe that black people were less intelligent than white people. To them, Banneker's intelligence was not normal for a black person.

Black scientists continued to disprove the myth of black inferiority during the next century. African American inventors exhibited their work at two international expositions, one in 1895 and the other the 1900 event in Paris. These fairs, which were designed to display scientific and cultural progress, demonstrated the ingenuity of African Americans to people throughout the world. Around the same time, black zoologist Charles Henry Turner and marine biologist Ernest Everett Just published their work in professional journals, a mark of distinction in their fields.

The early 1900s saw only a few black scientists employed in laboratories. World War II, however, forced scientists of all colors to work together on a broader scale. In the 1940s, black and white scientists put aside their racial differences to pursue a common goal: building the atomic bomb.

When the war ended, African American scientists felt the sting of prejudice once again. Top institutions would not hire them, and they

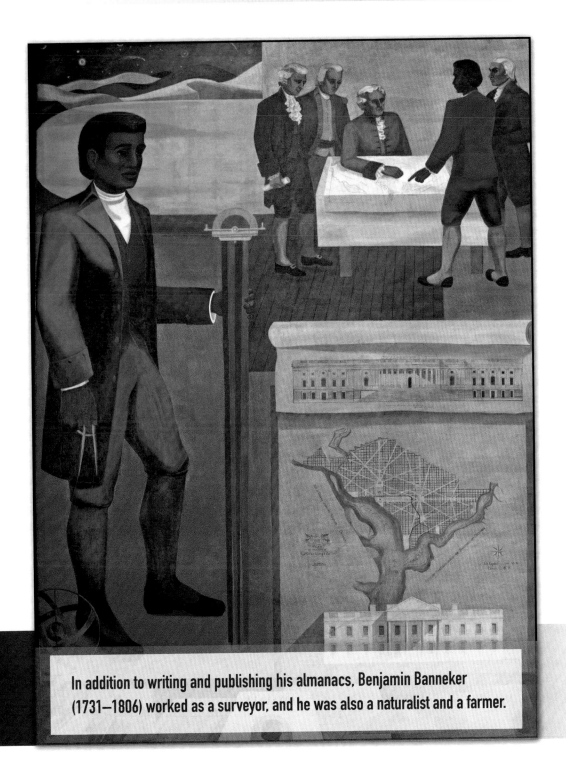

In addition to writing and publishing his almanacs, Benjamin Banneker (1731–1806) worked as a surveyor, and he was also a naturalist and a farmer.

were rarely allowed to attend national science conventions, which were often held in segregated hotels. In a field that depended on teamwork and the exchange of ideas, black scientists were at a great disadvantage.

FIGHTING FOR EQUAL EDUCATION

Perhaps the most important obstacle for blacks in science was the practice of separating students according to race (segregation). Even George Washington Carver, a brilliant student and avid learner, was denied admission to a university after the school's president learned that Carver was black. Carver later attended Simpson College in Iowa. Similarly, college advisors discouraged top-notch chemist Percy Lavon Julian from continuing into graduate school in 1920

Saint-Dominique in Washington, DC, was the first school to integrate its students following the *Brown v Board of Education* decision.

due to the dismal job situation for black professors. Years later, Julian developed a successful new treatment for arthritis.

Fortunately for Julian, Carver, and others, institutions such as Howard University, Morehouse College, Fisk University, and Tuskegee Institute emerged to give black scientists a place to study and teach. Over the years, historically black colleges became increasingly sophisticated. Yet they lacked the funds to support scientific research. Black professors often went without lab equipment and supplies with which to teach and experiment. When Carver arrived at Tuskegee in 1896, he found a barren plot of land on which to grow his crops.

In 1954 the US Supreme Court ruled against segregation in elementary schools in *Brown v. Board of Education, Topeka, Kansas*. Although the ruling did not force colleges or universities to desegregate, minority Americans were determined to hasten the change. Black scientists joined other citizens in demonstrations demanding equality. As a result, universities began to open their doors to minorities. A career in science was slowly becoming a reality for African Americans.

In 1972 the American Association for the Advancement of Science (AAAS) founded "Opportunities in Science," a program dedicated to attracting minorities to the field. Since then, other organizations have started similar programs. While these programs have had some success over the years, African Americans remain underrepresented in science. Thirteen out of every one hundred Americans are black. Yet, only eight out of every one hundred American college students who graduate with a degree in science or engineering are African American. At the graduate level, four out of one hundred doctoral degrees are awarded to black scientists and engineers. Society still has much work to do if it wants equal opportunities for everyone.

CHAPTER TWO

ONE INVENTION AT A TIME

Determined to achieve success, many black scientists and inventors have had to brave slavery, segregation, racism, and sexism. Profiled here are seven men and women who are not as widely known as George Washington Carver or Mae Jemison—featured later in this volume—but whose contributions to science and technology greatly enhanced the lives of thousands.

LEWIS TEMPLE

Lewis Temple (1800–1854) was born in Richmond, Virginia. Around 1830 he settled in New Bedford, Massachusetts, and began a career in metalworking.

During the 1800s, whale oil, whalebone, and whale meat were important trade goods. Dozens of whaling ships set out from New Bedford every year to hunt for whales. At his blacksmith shop, Temple made and repaired equipment for these ships.

Whaling was dangerous and difficult work. Crews chased whales in small boats until the men were close enough to spear the whales

Whalers try to harpoon a bowhead whale in this illustration.

with harpoons tied to long ropes. The triangular tip of the harpoon would strike and sink into the whale's blubber. As the injured whale tried to escape, it dragged the boat behind it.

When the whale tired, the crew moved in for the kill. Too often, however, the whale lurched around so much that the harpoon slipped out of the hole the tip had made in the whale's skin, and the whale got away.

When Temple learned about the problem from whalers who visited his shop, he set about making a better harpoon. In 1848 he devised a harpoon tip that flipped sideways and locked into place. Known as the Temple toggle iron, it had a major impact on the whaling industry, and New Bedford's whaleship owners prospered. In 1987 the city of New Bedford honored Temple with a life-size statue in front of the New Bedford Free Public Library.

15

REBECCA LEE
AND REBECCA J. COLE

African American women practiced the healing arts from their earliest days in America. Nevertheless, medical schools in the United States did not admit African Americans or women until well into

the 1800s. Rebecca Lee (1840–1881) and Rebecca J. Cole (1846–1922) challenged those barriers.

As a young woman, Rebecca Lee worked as a nurse in Massachusetts before entering the New England Female Medical College, a school in Boston that had recently opened to allow women to earn a medical degree (MD). In 1864 she

The New York Infirmary for Women and Children was created in 1857 by Drs. Elizabeth and Emily Blackwell and Dr. Marie Zakrzewska. The infirmary had grown from a small dispensary started by Elizabeth Blackwell in 1853.

became the first African American "Doctoress of Medicine." After the Civil War, Lee took her practice to Richmond, Virginia, where she spent many years caring for newly freed people.

Rebecca J. Cole was the second black woman physician in the United States. A native of Philadelphia, she received her medical degree from the Woman's Medical College of Pennsylvania in 1867.

Cole devoted her medical practice to helping the poor. For many years, she worked at the New York Infirmary for Women and Children, a hospital run entirely by women doctors. She visited families in city slums to teach them hygiene and baby care. Her work also took her to Columbia, South Carolina.

Returning later to Philadelphia, she opened the Women's Directory Center, which gave medical and legal aid to poor women and children. In the last years of her life, she worked as the superintendent of the Home for Destitute Colored Women and Children in Washington, DC. Her long career spanned fifty years.

CHARLES HENRY TURNER

As a young boy in Ohio, Charles Turner (1867–1923) loved bugs. After earning bachelor's and master's degrees in biology at the University of Cincinnati, he began teaching in black high schools and colleges in the South. In his spare time, he studied ants, bees, moths, and spiders with a microscope and homemade equipment.

He discovered that bees choose flowers by their odor and color, that insects not only can hear but can also tell high notes from low ones, and that moths can learn to respond to new dangers. He published these findings in scientific journals. In 1907 the University of Chicago awarded him a doctorate in zoology.

Turner's work became widely respected in the United States and Europe. In addition to his teaching and research, Turner also shared his love of biology by writing nature stories for children.

ERNEST EVERETT JUST

Following his mother's advice to "be the very best you can be," sixteen-year-old Ernest Everett Just (1883–1941) left Charleston, South Carolina, to study at Kimball Union Academy in New Hampshire and later at Dartmouth College. A top student, he earned special honors in his favorite subject—zoology.

Ernest Everett Just was one of the first black scientists to gain global recognition.

After college, Just taught at Howard University in Washington, DC. During summer vacations, he began working toward a PhD, but even before completing his degree from the University of Chicago in 1916, he published several papers in scientific journals.

Just's research focused on how cells reproduce. His experiments on the egg cells of marine animals led to new ideas about the early stages of growth. His innovative work attracted invitations from the best research laboratories in Europe. During the 1930s, he spent most of his time working in Berlin, Germany; Naples, Italy; and Paris, France. He eventually published more than sixty scientific papers and two books.

ROGER ARLINER YOUNG

When Virginia native Roger Arliner Young (1889–1964) took her first science course at Howard University, her teacher was Ernest Everett Just. Although he gave her only a C, he encouraged her to pursue a career in science.

After graduating in 1923, Young began teaching zoology at Howard and saving money for graduate school. She received her master's degree from the University of Chicago in 1926. Over the next ten years, she spent summers doing research with Just at the Marine Biological Laboratory in Woods Hole, Massachusetts. Experts praised her work on the effects of radiation on sea urchin eggs.

Young hoped to begin doctoral studies at Chicago in 1929. However, overworked and worried about her lack of money and her mother's health, she failed her qualifying exams. Then, in 1936, Howard fired her for missing classes. Young, however, did not give up. She eventually enrolled at the University of Pennsylvania to work on her PhD.

In 1940 Young became the first African American woman to receive a PhD in zoology. For the rest of her life, she taught at black colleges in North Carolina, Texas, Louisiana, and Mississippi.

RUTH ELLA MOORE

Ruth Ella Moore (1889–1964) grew up in Columbus, Ohio, and studied at Ohio State University. She earned a bachelor's degree in 1926 and a master's the following year.

In 1933 she became the first African American woman to receive a doctorate in microbiology. For her doctoral dissertation, she studied *tubercle bacillus,* the bacterium that causes tuberculosis. Interested in public health problems, Moore focused her research on both bacteria and blood grouping.

She spent her teaching career at Howard University College of Medicine, where she became the first African American woman to chair a department of a medical school in the United States. For twelve years, she was acting head and head of the Department of Bacteriology, Preventive Medicine, and Public Health.

CHAPTER THREE

NECESSITY IS THE MOTHER OF INVENTION

M adam C. J. Walker began her life as Sarah Breedlove. The fifth of six children, she was born on December 23, 1867, two years after the end of the American Civil War. Her parents, Owen and Minerva Breedlove, had been slaves but were living as "freemen," working as sharecroppers on their former master's plantation. In return for laboring twelve hours a day under the hot sun, they received a share of the cotton harvest. Unfortunately, the money they earned from selling their cotton was usually less than what they spent on equipment and supplies. As a result, Sarah's family was very poor. To earn a little extra money, Sarah helped her mother raise chickens and sell eggs. She and her sister also laundered clothes for "white folk," using big wooden tubs set out in their front yard.

OVERCOMING HARDSHIPS

When Sarah was seven years old, she found herself sitting on the step of her family's shack in Delta, Louisiana, scratching in the dusty earth with a stick. Tears trickled down her cheeks. "What

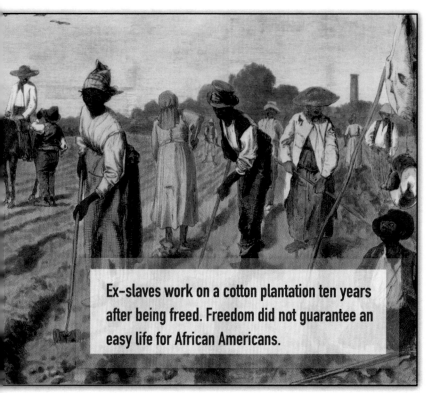

Ex-slaves work on a cotton plantation ten years after being freed. Freedom did not guarantee an easy life for African Americans.

will become of me?" she wondered aloud. An epidemic had taken her parents' lives, as often happened to poor African Americans who had little access to doctors or hospitals in the late 1800s. So Sarah, her sister, and her four brothers became orphans.

After her parents' deaths, Sarah worked on the plantation for three more years. But when her brother Alex moved across the Mississippi River to Vicksburg, Mississippi, and that year's cotton crop failed, Sarah and her sister, Louvenia, were not able to make enough money to keep their home. Forced to move, they, too, fled to Vicksburg.

In Vicksburg, Louvenia once again found work doing laundry, and Sarah helped. Not long afterward, Louvenia married, but her husband was a cruel and angry man. Sarah hated living with them in their crowded shack. At the age of fourteen, Sarah left and married a hardworking man named Moses McWilliams. When she was seventeen years old, she gave birth to her only child, a daughter, whom she named Lelia. Three years later, Sarah's husband died in an accident.

Sarah did not want to move back in with her sister, so when friends suggested that she could earn good money in St. Louis, Missouri, she and Lelia boarded a riverboat and headed north. Upon arriving in St. Louis, Sarah joined the Methodist Episcopal Church. Its members helped her get settled and find work as a washerwoman.

Although she still worked from sunup to sundown, Sarah was proud that she was able to set aside money for Lelia to attend college. At the time, very few black women received university training. She eventually saved enough to send her daughter to Knoxville College in Tennessee.

Sarah worked hard for many years and earned very little money. As a result of her hard life and poor diet, she developed a medical condition called alopecia. Her short, naturally curly hair began to fall out. To make matters worse, black women like Sarah often

Knoxville College was created in 1875 to provide a quality education to African Americans after the Civil War.

used hair products such as Kinkilla, La Creole Hair Restorer, and Queen Pomade. Some of these products contained harsh chemicals that burned the scalp. Women also ironed their hair and used hot metal combs to straighten it, causing it to become extremely dry and break off, sometimes in large clumps.

Thick, beautiful hair was important to Sarah. She did not like the way her short, patchy hair made her look or feel. She prayed to God it would not fall out anymore. One night Sarah had a dream about special ingredients, oils and creams, which could be made from plants. She believed the ingredients in her dream would improve her hair. The next morning, Sarah began to search out ingredients such as tetter salve and sulfur petrolatum to make hair-care products for black women. She began testing them on herself.

In 1905, after learning of her brother Alex's death, Sarah moved to Denver to be near his wife and four daughters. When she arrived, she had only one dollar and fifty cents in her purse. During the day, she worked as a cook for

Madam C. J. Walker was the first female entrepreneur in the world to become a millionaire.

Mr. E. L. Scholtz, owner of the largest pharmacy in the city. At night, using a homemade laboratory she had set up in a rented attic room, Sarah mixed and remixed hair-care formulas. Though her spelling was far from perfect, she took careful notes, recording the exact amounts of each ingredient used.

Over time, Sarah invented five reliable products. Her own hair began to grow back, and she started making plans to sell her hair tonics to other black women across the country. She began her business by going door-to-door and placing ads in newspapers. At about the same time, Charles Joseph Walker came to visit Sarah in Denver. She had known him in St. Louis and was happy to see him again. They married in 1906, so Sarah Breedlove changed her name to Madam C. J. Walker.

The term *Madam* sounded important. Sarah and Charles thought it would help her sell more products, and they were right. Her Vegetable Shampoo, Wonderful Hair Grower, and Glossine Hair Oil became so popular that Sarah was able to hire other women to demonstrate and sell her products door-to-door. Black women during Sarah's time had few rights and little status. They could not vote or own property and were prohibited from using certain theaters, hotels, and restaurants. Many depended on their husbands for money. Working as sales agents for the newly established Madam C. J. Walker Manufacturing Company allowed these women to earn a good income in a respected occupation.

UNPRECEDENTED SUCCESS

Sales of Madam Walker's products grew quickly, so Sarah moved the company to Pittsburgh, Pennsylvania, because its well-developed

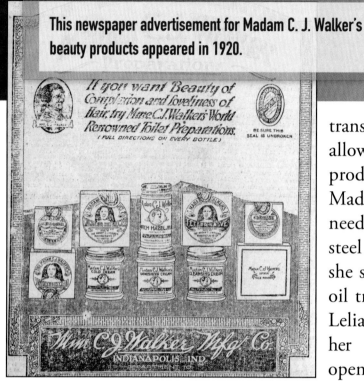

This newspaper advertisement for Madam C. J. Walker's beauty products appeared in 1920.

transportation system allowed her to ship her products more easily. Madam Walker also needed Pittsburgh's steel to make the comb she sold with her hair-oil treatment. She and Lelia, who changed her name to A'Lelia, opened a training school for sales agents. They charged twenty-five dollars but offered scholarships to women who could not pay the tuition. By 1908 the company was earning four hundred dollars a week, had hired nearly one hundred sales agents, and had opened beauty shops across the nation.

Madam Walker stayed only two years in Pittsburgh. In 1910 she relocated the company to Indianapolis, Indiana, then the country's largest inland manufacturing center. She built a new headquarters—a modern, one-block square building that included a Greek-style theater, a lunchroom, a drugstore, and a beauty parlor as well as the factory and office space. This building was the first of many contributions Madam Walker made to the cultural life of Indianapolis.

Madam Walker enjoyed sharing her money and her time. She made generous donations to many organizations, including the National Association for the Advancement of Colored People (NAACP). She funded scholarships for needy students and built homes for the elderly. Repeatedly, Madam Walker spoke out on behalf of her race. "This is the greatest country under the sun," she once said, "but we must not let our love of country, our patriotic loyalty, cause us to abate one whit in our protest against wrong and injustice."

After her divorce from Charles Walker in 1912 and her subsequent move to Villa Lewaro, her New York mansion, Madam Walker continued to promote her special interests as well as her company. Resting little, she eventually developed high blood pressure, and while in St. Louis on business, she became seriously ill. She was rushed home in a private railroad car, but she did not recover, and on May 25, 1919, Madam C. J. Walker died at fifty-one years of age.

When Madam Walker died, she was a millionaire. Her company was earning a quarter of a million dollars per year and employed twenty-five thousand women. During her lifetime, she was financially successful yet continued to believe that real success came from sharing with others. During a 1912 speech to the National Negro Business League, she told the crowd, "My object in life is not simply to make money for myself but to use part of what I make in trying to help others." Even now, although her company is no longer in operation, and Madam Walker has been dead for nearly a century, she is still remembered for her successes in improving the lives of countless black Americans. She never allowed herself to become defeated by hardship. On the contrary, she rose above it, achieving great wealth and success in business and becoming a powerful role model for women of all races and social classes.

CHAPTER FOUR

THE WIZARD OF TUSKEGEE

George Washington Carver (c. 1865–1943) often quoted his favorite Bible verse: "Behold, I have given you every herb bearing seed, which is upon the face of all the earth . . . to you it shall be for meat." This verse provided Carver not only with inspiration, but also with purpose. Carver wrote that "it has always been the one great ideal of my life to be of the greatest good to the greatest number of 'my people' possible." And he did that with the lowly peanut.

An orphaned, somewhat sickly child, Carver grew up in Missouri under the care of his parents' former owners, the Carvers. At age ten, he chose to travel to a neighboring community to

George Washington Carver

attend a school for blacks. To support himself, he took a job working for a black family in return for room and board.

Carver was naturally curious and had an intense desire to learn. He especially liked plants and flowers, studying and sketching them whenever he could. His perseverance and determination led him to become the first African American to earn an advanced degree in scientific agriculture. When Booker T. Washington, founder of Alabama's Tuskegee Normal and Industrial Institute (now Tuskegee University), offered him a position as director of the Department of Agricultural Research in 1896, Carver accepted. The Institute then became his home and the site of his experiments.

Booker T. Washington

Everywhere he looked, Carver saw poor black farmers with exhausted soil and stunted crops. Years of planting only cotton had robbed the soil of vital nutrients. To replenish the soil, Carver advocated crop rotation and developed a special species of cotton. Because Carver's hybrid cotton grew quickly, farmers could pick it before insects destroyed it.

But people could not eat cotton, and what the farmers and their families needed was a crop that was edible and, at the same time, replaced the nutrients used by cotton. Carver suggested peanuts, an easy source of protein and other nutrients. People were upset by this

Carver's students gained hands-on experience in his lab at the Tuskegee Institute.

suggestion. Did he expect them to eat livestock feed? At the time, people thought that was the only use for peanuts.

To counter their concerns, Carver developed more than three hundred peanut products: milk, cream, cheese, soap, medicines, wood stain, dyes, even facial powder. Of course, his most popular product was peanut butter, although he was not actually the first to invent it. The uses he created for the lowly peanut offered such potential that in 1919 a group of businessmen formed the United Peanut Association of America to make peanuts profitable.

But Carver did not stop with the peanut. He also developed hundreds of uses for the soybean and the sweet potato. Today he is considered the father of chemurgy, the science of creating new agricultural products.

CHAPTER FIVE

THE SKY'S THE LIMIT

A t the National Aeronautics and Space Administration (NASA), the opportunities for black scientists are out of this world. The following six stellar scientists broke barriers and proved that with hard work and determination, the sky's the limit—and sometimes, not even the sky could limit what could be achieved in science.

On August 30, 1983, "Guy" Bluford (1942–) became the first African American in space, serving as a mission specialist onboard the shuttle *Challenger*.

As a boy, Bluford worked hard to keep up with others in school. But he went on to college and earned three degrees in aerospace engineering. Later, as a pilot in the Air Force, Bluford flew 144 combat missions over Vietnam. In 1978, when Bluford applied to become an astronaut, NASA chose him from among eight thousand applicants.

As Bluford sped through the atmosphere aboard *Challenger* that night after takeoff in 1983, he was giddy with excitement. "I laughed and giggled all the way up," he told a reporter. "It was such a fun ride."

Bluford was a mission specialist aboard the 1983 *Challenger* mission

KATHERINE JOHNSON

Katherine Johnson (1918–) began working at NASA as a mathematician in 1953. At that time, the only "computers" were people who solved problems using pencil and paper. Over the next thirty-three years, NASA's technology improved, but Johnson's job remained complex: to calculate the flight paths of NASA's spacecraft.

In 1969 Johnson's calculations helped land Neil Armstrong and Buzz Aldrin on the moon. For this mission, Johnson performed four sets of computations: the flight of *Apollo 11* to the moon, the path of the landing module to the moon's surface, the flight of the mod-

This photograph of Katherine Johnson was taken at NASA's Langley Research Center in 1966.

ule back to *Apollo 11*, and the return path of *Apollo 11* to Earth. Johnson also made a map of the stars that the astronauts used during their flight to see where they were every step of the way.

VANCE MARCHBANKS

If astronaut John Glenn's heart had skipped a beat while he orbited Earth in 1962, Vance Marchbanks (1905–1988) would have known right away. A flight surgeon for NASA, Marchbanks was responsible for monitoring Glenn's health during this historic flight.

Glenn could not have been in better hands. Before joining NASA, Marchbanks had served in the Air Force for twenty-three years. There, he earned several medals for his bravery and research. In 1962, when Glenn lifted off aboard *Friendship 7*, Marchbanks watched from a tracking station in Nigeria, Africa. From there, Marchbanks monitored Glenn's vital signs using reports sent by the electronic sensing devices in Glenn's body suit.

Later, Marchbanks helped design the space suits, backpacks, and monitoring systems for the Apollo moon missions.

PATRICIA COWINGS

At NASA, Patricia Cowings (1948–) is known as the "Baroness of Barf." That is because she makes astronauts sick so she can learn how to make them feel better again.

Cowings is a psychophysiologist, a scientist who studies how thoughts and emotions affect the body. Her job is to train astronauts to avoid space adaptation syndrome (SAS), a condition similar to motion sickness that occurs when humans experience zero gravity.

Under Cowings's watch, astronauts dress in body suits that measure their temperature, blood pressure, heart rate, and breathing. An instrument called an oscilloscope displays these readings to the astronauts as waves of light. By watching and responding to the light waves, astronauts learn to control the symptoms of SAS. Their final test is a spin through the "vomit comet," a zero-gravity flight simulator. If the astronauts emerge feeling well, Cowings knows her job is done.

GEORGE CARRUTHERS

Born in 1939, George Carruthers built his first telescope when he was ten, using cardboard and lenses he had ordered through the mail. He later earned degrees in physics and aeronautical and astronomical engineering and became an expert in ultraviolet (UV) radiation. UV rays are the invisible wavelengths of light just beyond violet in the electromagnetic spectrum.

At NASA, Carruthers designed a camera called a spectrograph that could take "pictures" of ultraviolet rays. In 1972 the crew of *Apollo 16* used Carruthers's spectrograph to record more than two hundred images from the surface of the moon. These images included newly discovered stars and nebulae, or clouds of gas or dust, as well as images of the earth's atmosphere that helped scientists study new ways to control air pollution.

Mae Jemison steps out of a training jet at the Kennedy Space Center in September 1992.

MAE C. JEMISON

As a child, Mae Jemison (1956–) preferred cold winter nights—they were the best for viewing stars. But it was not until Jemison became the first black woman in space that she discovered the best way to stargaze.

Jemison enjoyed reading science-fiction books when she was young. But she was constantly frustrated that girls never played the leading roles. Although Jemison did well in school and was admitted to Stanford University in 1973, many people doubted that a black girl could become a scientist. Jemison proved them wrong. She later completed medical school and spent two years in Africa as a medical officer with the Peace Corps. In 1987 NASA invited Jemison to become an astronaut. Five years later, as she peered out the window of the shuttle *Endeavour*, Jemison remembered the little girl in Chicago who had admired the stars.

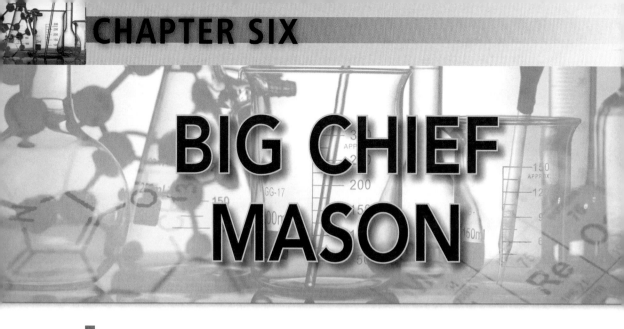

CHAPTER SIX

BIG CHIEF MASON

I n October 1914, fire chiefs from across the country saw an un-usual demonstration in New Orleans, Louisiana. A dark-skinned man introduced as Big Chief Mason put a canvas hood over his head, walked into a smoke-filled tent, and closed the flap behind him. The smoke came from a burning mixture of tar, manure, and other foul-smelling substances. The New Orleans *Times-Picayune* re-ported that the smoke was "the most evil-smelling imaginable" and "thick enough to strangle an elephant."

The man stayed inside the tent for about twenty minutes. When he came out, he removed his hood and said he felt "as good as new."

Representatives from the National Safety Device Company of Cleveland gave this demonstration to advertise their safety hood. The hood connected to two hoses that joined in the back and reached to the ground. Because smoke rises, there is usually a layer of clean air near the ground. The hood let its wearer breathe this clean air.

Big Chief Mason was actually Garrett Augustus Morgan, the African American inventor of the safety hood. Morgan's hood was an early version of the gas mask. He called it a "breathing device." Later "Style Two" models carried their own air supply in a pouch.

Garett A. Morgan

Improved masks protected American soldiers during poison gas attacks in World War I.

Why did Morgan use an Indian disguise to demonstrate the hood? He had learned that some people would not buy a product invented by a black man. Fire departments in Yonkers, New York; Cleveland and Akron, Ohio; and Los Angeles, California, did buy and use Morgan's hood, however.

The hood drew national attention when a pocket of gas exploded in a Cleveland Waterworks tunnel under Lake Erie on July 24, 1916. Many workers were trapped in the tunnel. Garrett Morgan and his brother Frank arrived on the scene with several Style Two hoods. With two volunteers, they entered the smoky tunnel and began carrying out survivors. Others soon joined them. In total, thirty-two lives were saved.

This rescue put Morgan and his hood in the public eye. Sadly, when people learned that an African American had invented the hood, many decided not to buy it. But Morgan would not let that keep him down.

THE ACCIDENTAL HAIR PRODUCT

Garrett Morgan was born in Claysville, Kentucky, in 1877. He attended school through the sixth grade. When he was fourteen years old, he went to Cincinnati, Ohio, and worked as a handyman. Later, he settled in Cleveland, where he repaired sewing machines for a living. By 1909 he had his own tailoring shop employing thirty-two people. While trying to develop a polish for sewing machine needles, Morgan stumbled onto something else.

This undated photograph shows a nine-foot water tunnel under Lake Erie in Ohio. The possibility of gas explosions and collapses made this work rather dangerous.

Sewing machine needles moved at a high speed. Sometimes a needle became so hot that it scorched the fabric it was sewing. One night, Morgan was working on a polish to lubricate the needles and thus reduce the heat. He wiped his hands on a piece of pony fur cloth.

Later he noticed that the curly fuzz on the cloth was straight where he had wiped his hands. He tried his polish on a neighbor's Airedale. The dog's wiry coat also became straight. Morgan then tried the polish on his own hair. He realized that he had discovered something valuable. He made a hair-straightening cream out of his polish and sold it. The income from the hair cream enabled Morgan to develop his safety hood, which he began working on in 1910.

Morgan had enough money to buy a car, too. The number of automobiles in Cleveland was growing, and one day Morgan saw a car collide with a horse and carriage. He began to think of a way to control traffic.

KEEPING ROADS SAFE

In 1923 he patented a traffic signal for use at four-way intersections. Depending on which way the signal faced, drivers saw the word "Stop" or "Go" on its extended arms and top section. When a policeman turned a crank, the arms lifted to show "Stop" in all directions, allowing pedestrians to cross the streets.

Then the policeman turned the arms and top section a quarter turn and lowered the arms. Now traffic could flow in the other direction. Morgan's traffic signal was widely used until it was superseded by the modern three-color electric traffic light.

This is the patent drawing for Morgan's three-position traffic signal.

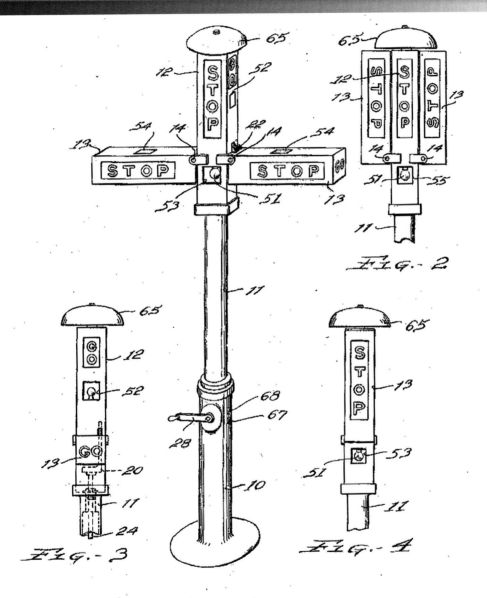

FIG.-1

FIG.-2

FIG.-3

FIG.-4

INVENTOR
Garrett A. Morgan,
By Bates & Macklin,
ATTORNEYS

Morgan was actively involved in public life. He founded the *Cleveland Call,* a weekly newspaper, in 1920, and was a charter member of the Cleveland Association of Colored Men. (This later became part of the National Association for the Advancement of Colored People.) He ran unsuccessfully for city council in 1931.

This 1913 illustration shows the dangers, such as oblivious pedestrians and playing children, a driver faces when out on the road. Morgan's traffic light helped reduce the number of car accidents.

DON'T BLAME THE MOTORIST FOR ALL THE AUTOMOBILE ACCIDENTS IN CITY STREETS.   LOOK AT SOME OF THE THINGS HE IS UP AGAINST:

There are the boys, for instance, who use an asphalt thoroughfare for a ball-ground, and who never watch anything but the ball. And there are the little devils who dart out in front of you and dare you to run over them. There is the man who makes a "Dutch crossing" in and out of traffic; the chap who leaves a trolley-car and comes around behind it; and the absent-minded mortal who looks neither up nor down, but steps off the curb intent upon his newspaper. And there are others—yet the motorist always gets the blame when anybody is hurt! The reckless pedestrian is as bad as the reckless motorist.

In 1943 Morgan was diagnosed with glaucoma, and his eyesight steadily declined. He died in 1963 at the age of eighty-six.

TRUE PIONEERS

From soil-preserving crop rotation methods and innovative beauty products to the creation of tools and inventions that simplified and improved life, African American inventors and scientists have revolutionized daily life in the modern world. They overcame injustice, prejudice, and inequality to triumph in every American field of endeavor, from agriculture to the space program. Their ability to transcend the culture of their time and become innovators and scientists shows that they truly were pioneers.

GLOSSARY

attorney A lawyer; a person who is hired or appointed to conduct business on someone else's behalf.

destitute Lacking money or resources or living in extreme poverty.

epidemic An outbreak of a virus or infectious disease in a community.

evaporator A tool or machine that has the job of removing liquid from matter.

exposition A public showing or exhibition of something, such as art or new technology.

hybrid The offspring of a plant or animal in which different species or varieties have been combined to create a new plant or animal.

microbiology The study of microorganisms.

nutrient One of many elements in food or soil that provides the materials an organism needs to live and grow.

page A young person who attends a person in authority, such as a congress person.

patent A government document that gives a person or company exclusive rights to the making, using, or selling of a particular item.

refining The process of removing impurities from something.

segregation The act of setting someone or something apart from other people or things.

survey A series of questions used to collect information about something or someone or a group of people or things.

telegraph A system that uses a wire to send signals over a distance.

vacuum A space that has no matter.

zoology The study of animals.

BOOKS

Litwin, Laura Baskes. *The Life of Benjamin Banneker*. Berkeley Heights, NJ: Enslow Publishers, 2014.

Ploscariu, Iemima. *Mae Carol Jemison: Astronaut and Educator*. Minneapolis, MN: Essential Library, 2017.

Rich, Mari. *Inventors*. Broomall, PA: Mason Crest, 2016.

Shetterly, Margot Lee. *Hidden Figures: The American Dream and the Untold Story of the Black Women Mathematicians Who Helped Win the Space Race*. New York, NY: William Morrow, 2016.

Washburne, Sophie. *African American Inventors: Overcoming Challenges to Change America*. New York, NY: Lucent Books, 2017.

WEBSITES

The Faces of Science: African Americans in the Sciences
webfiles.uci.edu/mcbrown/display/faces.html
Search profiles of African American scientists by name or profession.

National Geographic Kids, Black Inventors and Pioneers of Science
kids.nationalgeographic.com/explore/science/black-inventors-and -pioneers-of-science/#black-scientist-jemison.jpg
Photos and brief biographical blurbs highlight some of the African American pioneers in the areas of science and innovation.

Scholastic, Famous African American Inventors
teacher.scholastic.com/activities/bhistory/inventors/index.htm
Read about the lives and accomplishments of fourteen African American inventors.

INDEX